EMERGING AI TECHNOLOGY
A GLIMPSE INTO THE FUTURE

DWAYNE ROBINSON

INTRODUCTION
FACING AI WITH CLARITY AND CONFIDENCE

The headlines about artificial intelligence are everywhere—and they rarely sound friendly to people or small businesses. If you're worried about your job becoming obsolete or your company falling behind, you're not alone. That concern is genuine. It's also the reason I wrote this book.

AI isn't a distant idea anymore—it's here. It screens applications, suggests routes, and helps clinicians spot risks earlier. That progress raises fair questions: Where do people fit? What happens to our jobs? Can small teams compete when software can do so much?

This book is a direct conversation with you—the professional, team lead, or business owner—about moving from fear to confident action. We'll acknowledge the risks, but we'll do it with practical optimism and a clear plan.

A Tool, not a Threat

The most productive way to see AI is as a powerful tool that amplifies human talent—not a replacement for it. Its real value is in removing friction: automating repetitive steps so people can focus on strategy, creativity, and relationships.

Early in my career, when I founded Vision Systems & Technology, Inc. (VSTI), our teams supported mission needs across the U.S. Intelligence Community. We didn't "replace" great engineers with automation. We built tools that enabled great engineers to work faster and more effectively. That's the opportunity in front of us now: augmentation, not obsolescence.

A Practical Plan You Can Use

Control starts with a simple operating model you can apply to any AI system you encounter. You don't need a technical background to use it. The framework is:

Understand – Question – Act (UQA)

1. Understand: What exactly is this system doing, in plain language? Where does it excel, and where does it struggle?
2. Question: Who built it and for what purpose? What data trained it? How is it tested for fairness, reliability, and safety? Who is accountable for outcomes?
3. Act: What concrete steps will we take to adopt AI responsibly at work or in our community? What safeguards do we need?

UQA puts you back behind the wheel. You move from reacting

to headlines to making deliberate choices about how technology serves your goals.

A Clear-Eyed, Human-First Perspective

We'll take a balanced view—celebrating promising results and learning from missteps. In healthcare, for example, AI has shown considerable promise in detecting diabetic eye disease, enabling clinicians to intervene earlier. At the same time, we've seen cautionary cases where systems offered unsafe recommendations. The point isn't to fear or to hype; it's to use evidence and judgment to guide decisions.

When I led teams through high-pressure proposal processes, we followed the same principle: use technology to eliminate low-value friction so people can perform at their best. That human-focused approach cut down time spent on repetitive tasks, enabling experts to concentrate on strategy, quality, and results. The same mindset applies to individuals and business owners navigating AI today.

What You'll Gain

By the end of this book, you will be able to:

- Shift from anxiety to action, seeing AI as a co-pilot that extends your strengths.
- Identify where AI can genuinely help your work or operations—and where it can't.
- Recognize common risk patterns—such as bias, privacy, and misinformation—and manage them responsibly.
- Use the UQA framework to make confident, values-aligned decisions about adoption.

How to Use This Book

We'll build understanding step by step:

- Chapter 1 gives a practical context—how we got here and what history teaches us.
- Chapter 2 explains current capabilities and limits in plain language.
- Chapter 3 examines real-world applications across various industries and daily life, highlighting trade-offs.
- Chapter 4 addresses serious risks and outlines strategies for reducing harm while maintaining accountability.
- Chapter 5 looks ahead to near-term possibilities, focusing on responsible and human-centered adoption.

You'll also find short "Reader's Toolkit" sections—simple questions and checklists you can apply immediately.

READER'S TOOLKIT: FIRST STEPS FOR WORRIED READERS

Mindset Shift

- Identify one repetitive task you do every week. If AI handled it, what higher-value work could you do?
- Reframe "replacement" as "redeployment." Where could you and your team add more value if routine steps were automated?

Before Adopting a Tool

- What problem will this solution address, and how will we measure its success?
- How will a human stay "in the loop" for important decisions?

- Who is accountable if the system produces a poor or biased outcome?

AI is not destiny; it's design. The outcome depends on how we choose to build, deploy, and govern these tools. If you're ready to move from fear to clarity—and from clarity to action—you're in the right place. Let's begin.

CHAPTER ONE
UNDERSTANDING THE AI SHIFT — FROM POTENTIAL TO PARTNERSHIP

I f you are a business owner or a professional, the constant headlines about artificial intelligence can feel overwhelming. It is reasonable to worry about what this means for your job or your company. The truth is, AI did not arrive overnight; it has been evolving for decades. Understanding where it came from—and why it accelerated—helps you decide how to put it to work for you.

This chapter gives that perspective. We look back at the ideas and milestones that shaped AI not for a history lesson, but to provide you with a practical foundation. When you see the whole arc—including the setbacks—you can replace anxiety with a clear plan.

THE LONG ROAD TO TODAY'S AI

The idea of intelligent machines goes back to the mid-20th century. Early pioneers established the concept of "Artificial Intelligence" and examined how systems could think and solve problems. These early systems employed rules and logic, producing impressive demonstrations in structured areas, such as proofs and simple games. However, they struggled with the ambiguity and complexity of the real world. Computing power and data were limited. The vision was strong; the tools were not yet ready.

Learning from Setbacks

Enthusiasm cooled during what are now known as "AI winters," when expectations exceeded actual results. These cycles were humbling but valuable. The main lesson is that successful AI requires three key elements working in tandem: high-quality data, sufficient computing power to learn from it, and practical methods to measure performance in real-world situations. These lessons paved the way for sustainable progress.

THE THREE PILLARS OF MODERN AI

Modern AI emerged when three forces aligned:

1. Massive data - The growth of digital content, sensors, and connected devices created large training sets. Systems learned robust patterns in language, images, and behavior.

2. Powerful computing - Specialized hardware (such as GPUs) made it feasible to train deeper, more capable models at scale.

3. More innovative training methods, including improved learning techniques and architectures, have unlocked significant gains in vision, speech, and language tasks.

With those pillars in place, AI moved from lab promise to practical tools.

From Theory to Practical Tools

As those forces aligned, progress became visible in several ways: major leaps in image recognition, breakthroughs in learning complex strategies, and rapid advances in language understanding and generation. What matters for you is not the buzzwords—it is the shift from "someday" to "usable now."

In my own experience leading teams at Vision Systems & Technology, Inc. (VSTI), we saw this transition firsthand. Tools once treated as experiments began supporting real mission outcomes. The value was not in replacing experts, but in removing repetitive steps so specialists could focus on judgment, strategy, and quality. AI became the partner that cleared friction; people delivered the insight.

Four Lessons for Navigating What's Next

1. Progress is cumulative, not sudden.
   - Change arrives in phases. You have time to understand, adapt, and integrate thoughtfully.

2. Focus on outcomes, not hype.
   - Ground decisions in what works today. Look for proven use cases and clear benchmarks that align with your specific context.

3. AI is powerful—and bounded.
   - Systems reflect their training data and deployment context. Knowing your limits is essential for using AI effectively and safely.

4. You stay in the driver's seat.

○ Your choices—what to adopt, how to implement, which problems to solve—determine the outcome for your business or career.

YOUR PATH FORWARD: FROM FEAR TO ACTION

Today's AI is useful but imperfect. That mix creates space for leadership. Your domain knowledge and human judgment remain essential. The goal is not to compete with AI, but to partner with it—directing it toward the correct problems and standards, with people accountable for results.

By understanding this history, you can see AI for what it is: a powerful, practical tool that is ready to serve your goals when paired with responsible guardrails and a human-first mindset.

READER'S TOOLKIT — A CLEAR-EYED VIEW OF AI

1. What problem will this help us solve, and how will we measure success?
2. What data and computing made this possible—and would it work reliably in our environment?
3. Where are the human checkpoints—who reviews, who approves, who is accountable?
4. If the system fails, who will be affected, and how will we respond to the situation?

CHAPTER TWO
AI TODAY — A PRACTICAL SNAPSHOT OF YOUR NEW TOOLKIT

A I has transitioned from the research lab to practical use. For business owners and professionals, this is not a time for fear but a time for focus and resolve. Grasping what AI can and cannot do is the first step in turning disruption into an opportunity.

This chapter provides a clear overview of current AI capabilities, including where these systems add value, their limitations, and how to assess them with confidence. The aim is to give you practical insights, free from hype, so that you can see the way forward for your career and business.

WHERE AI CREATES OPPORTUNITY TODAY

Consider the following as case studies for using AI to improve your operations, rather than as threats to replace people.

- Conversational assistance: Voice and chat systems streamline customer support and internal workflows. They handle routine inquiries and information lookups, so your team can focus on higher-value problem-solving.

- Healthcare support: Algorithms act as a second set of eyes for clinicians, spotting patterns in medical images and data. Systems showing promise in detecting diabetic eye disease illustrate how AI can augment expert judgment.
- Financial services: AI helps detect fraud and assess financial risk, strengthening security and operational efficiency. For consequential decisions, human oversight remains essential.
- Transportation and logistics: Route optimization and traffic prediction offer a competitive edge for any business that moves goods. Full autonomy is domain-specific, but driver-assist features improve efficiency today.
- Recommendations and personalization: E-commerce and media platforms tailor customer experiences with the help of AI—balance personalization with discovery and user control.
- Manufacturing and quality: Vision systems identify defects in real-time; predictive maintenance minimizes downtime. These tools are most effective when integrated with frontline feedback.
- Education: Adaptive learning and tutoring aids support teachers and personalize instruction for students when guided by sound pedagogy.
- Climate and energy: Forecasting and optimization enable more efficient management of energy systems and more effective modeling of complex scenarios.

THE TECHNOLOGY DRIVING THIS PROGRESS

Several key advances have contributed to AI's recent leap in capability. Understanding them in plain language helps you spot opportunities.

- Deep learning: Trained on large datasets, these models learn patterns in images, speech, and text.
- Transformer architectures: A significant advance that improved how AI understands and generates human language; foundational for modern language tools.
- Vision breakthroughs: Landmark results in image recognition unlocked robust visual understanding for quality control and medical imaging support.
- Reinforcement learning: Systems learn through trial and error to master complex tasks, informing robotics and operations.
- Generative modeling: Models synthesize new text, images, audio, and code—powerful for creativity and productivity, with safeguards needed.

In my own work leading proposal operations, we utilize AI to draft compliant baselines and organize knowledge, allowing experts to focus on strategy, evidence, and clarity. The result is less friction for teams and stronger outcomes for clients.

PRAGMATIC BOUNDARIES TO RESPECT

Effective leaders know the limits of their tools. AI is powerful, but it is not magic. Acknowledging boundaries is essential for responsible use.

- Data dependence: AI reflects the training data it was

given. Biased or incomplete data yields biased or brittle behavior—ongoing monitoring matters.

- Robustness and generalization: Models that perform well in testing can struggle when faced with real-world variation. Always test in your actual context.
- Interpretability: Complex models can be hard to explain. For high-stakes uses, ensure transparency and auditability.
- Privacy and security: Strong data protection and governance are non-negotiable. Customers and employees must trust how data is handled.
- Ethics and safety: Responsible use requires attention to fairness, accountability, and meaningful human oversight—not just technical accuracy.

How to Evaluate AI Claims for Your Business

When you hear "AI-powered," look beyond the marketing and promotions. Ask for demonstrations using your own data in your environment. Seek clear benchmarks that match your goals, and demand a plan for human oversight in decisions that impact people, money, or safety.

Your Action Checklist

Use these questions to guide adoption:

- What specific, measurable business problem will this tool solve?
- How does the system perform with real, messy data from my operations—not just a clean demo?
- Who is the human in the loop, and how do they review, override, or appeal AI decisions?

- How are privacy, data security, and misuse risks addressed?

CHAPTER THREE
AI TRANSFORMING INDUSTRIES, EDUCATION, AND DAILY LIFE

Artificial Intelligence is no longer confined to labs or big tech campuses—it's in boardrooms, classrooms, homes, and clinics. What we're witnessing isn't a trend. It's a full-system shift.

This chapter examines how AI is actively transforming the core pillars of society—industry, education, daily life, and healthcare. But more than the 'how,' we'll dig into the 'so what.' What does this transformation mean for equity, access, and opportunity?

INDUSTRY: FROM EFFICIENCY TO INTELLIGENCE

In finance, AI isn't just predicting markets—it's determining who gets access to capital. Algorithms now drive high-frequency trading, flag fraud, and guide creditworthiness assessments. But when AI mirrors historical data, it can also reflect historical bias.

In manufacturing, we've moved from human hands to intelligent machines. AI-enabled robotics improve precision and productivity—but also reduce the need for headcount. The challenge isn't just adoption; it's inclusion. Are displaced workers being re-skilled or replaced?

Retail is more than shelf space—it's personalization at scale. AI tailors recommendations, predicts customer behavior, and automates logistics. That's good for margins, but we must also ask: what happens to workers behind the curtain of automation?

In the energy sector, AI optimizes grid systems and prevents outages through predictive maintenance. It's also accelerating the green transition. But equitable deployment must follow—rural communities and low-income areas can't be left behind.

EDUCATION: EQUITY THROUGH INNOVATION—OR AUTOMATION?

AI is unlocking new learning dimensions—through virtual and augmented reality, adaptive content, and real-time feedback. Students can travel through time, explore human anatomy, or solve global challenges from their desks.

But access is not automatic. Who gets the immersive tools? Who gets stuck with outdated software? AI-driven education must be rooted in justice—addressing bias in the curriculum, closing the digital divide, and enabling students with disabilities through assistive technology.

Virtual classrooms hold promise, but also widen the gap if connectivity is limited. The mission isn't just innovation—it's inclusion.

DAILY LIFE: INVISIBLE INFRASTRUCTURE, TANGIBLE IMPACT

From morning routines to midnight playlists, AI shapes our lives in ways we barely notice. Voice assistants organize schedules. Recommendation engines nudge behavior. Navigation tools recalibrate our day.

It's efficient, yes—but also increasingly persuasive. These systems learn us. The question is: who taught them? Whose data trained them? Responsible use means interrogating the unseen hands behind the automation.

Healthcare: Precision Meets Access

AI in healthcare is groundbreaking, enabling the diagnosis of conditions, the design of drugs, and the tailoring of treatment plans. Algorithms now read MRIs, scan pathology slides, and predict disease trajectories.

Yet, bias in datasets can result in missed diagnoses for marginalized populations. And AI without access is just a concept. Telemedicine, remote diagnostics, and personalized care must reach beyond zip codes and status.

The Moment We're In

We're not waiting for the future. We're living inside it. AI is already transforming how we work, learn, live, and heal. But transformation without intention can deepen disparities.

This moment calls for clarity, ethics, and courageous design. Not just to scale AI—but to shape it. And to ensure that every system it touches becomes more just, more human, and more accountable.

CHAPTER FOUR
THE SERIOUS RISKS OF AI: NAVIGATING THE ETHICAL LANDSCAPE

I f you're concerned about AI's impact on people and jobs, you're already thinking like a responsible leader. The right question isn't "Will AI replace us?" but "How can we use it without compromising our values, our people, and our customers?" This chapter emphasizes practical risk management, so AI becomes a reliable partner—not an unpredictable force.

AI is powerful and imperfect. Treat it that way. When we acknowledge risks early and design guardrails by default, we protect people, reduce surprises, and create space for the benefits to show up reliably.

Why Risks Matter for Your Business

Unchecked risks do real damage: to people (fairness, privacy, safety), to brand (trust and reputation), and to operations (cost, rework, and delay). Healthy skepticism is an asset. It keeps adoption focused on outcomes, accountability, and measurable improvement—not feature lists or hype.

Early in my proposal operations work, we strengthened results by introducing simple, disciplined practices: named ownership, traceability for claims, and a clear path to escalate concerns. Those same habits, when applied to AI, turn abstract "ethics" into everyday operating standards.

Four Common Risk Patterns (and What to Do About Them)

1. Bias and unfairness
   o What it is: Models learn from historical data. If the data reflects inequities, the system can reproduce or amplify them.
   o What to do: Define the intended use clearly. Test performance across relevant groups. Document known limits. Provide a manual review path for high-impact decisions.

2. Privacy and security
   o What it is: Training and deployment involve sensitive information. Weak controls can expose data or enable misuse.
   o What to do: Minimize data collected, restrict access, and log usage—separate environments for development vs. production. Treat privacy and security as non-negotiables.

3. Misinformation and overconfidence
   o What it is: Generative systems can produce fluent but incorrect content; predictive systems can be brittle under new conditions.
   o What to do: Require human review where accuracy matters. Mark AI-assisted content internally. For public-facing material, institute quality checks and escalation protocols.

4. Lack of Transparency and accountability
   - What it is: Black-box behavior makes it hard to explain decisions or resolve disputes.
   - What to do: Assign named owners for each use case. Keep records of data sources, intended use, known limits, and change history. Define an appeal path for users and customers.

PRACTICAL SAFEGUARDS YOU CAN IMPLEMENT NOW

- Problem-first scoping: Tie each AI use to a specific, measurable outcome (accuracy, cycle time, cost, equity). If the result is vague, pause.
- Human-in-the-loop by design: Decide when humans must review, approve, or override. Make this explicit for high-impact tasks (hiring, eligibility, safety, finance, healthcare, compliance).
- Evidence and traceability: Link claims to sources (past performance, metrics, documents). Track model versions and content origin to answer the question, "Where did this come from?"
- Real-world testing: Pilot with your data and workflows. Measure performance across scenarios and sub-groups. Monitor drift (performance changes over time).
- Change control: Treat prompts, training data, and content libraries like code. Minor tweaks can change outcomes: document changes and approvals.
- Clear user communication: If the AI supports a decision, clearly state so. Provide contact points for questions or appeals. Use plain language.

GOVERNANCE THAT BUILDS TRUST

Good governance is not bureaucracy—it is clarity. The aim is to make the correct behavior the easy behavior.

- Roles and responsibilities - Appoint an owner for each use of AI (not just the tool). Owners approve purpose, data sources, and deployment criteria.

- Risk tiering - Not all uses are equal. Classify by impact (people, dollars, safety). Higher tiers require stronger oversight and documentation.

- Review cadence - Schedule periodic checks (quarterly is a good start) to reassess performance, fairness, security, and user feedback. Sunset what no longer delivers value.

- Training and Awareness - Equip Your Team to Use AI Responsibly. Provide examples of good and bad usage. Make it easy to ask questions early.

In my teams, the combination of named ownership, short feedback loops, and simple documentation prevented problems from becoming crises. It kept us transparent with stakeholders and gave us confidence in our results.

- Putting Safeguards to Work: A Simple Operating Checklist
- Purpose. What are we solving, and how will we measure success?
- People. Who is accountable? Where are the human checkpoints?
- Data. What data is used, who has access, and how is it protected?

- Performance. How does it behave in our real-world cases and subgroups?
- Process. How will we monitor, retrain, and handle drift or failure?
- Transparency. What do users need to know? How do they ask questions or appeal?

A CULTURE THAT OUTLASTS THE HYPE

Tools change. Culture endures. You will outlast market noise if you build a culture that rewards clarity, safety, and measured improvement. Encourage your teams to speak up early, test assumptions, and propose better guardrails. The best indicator that your governance is effective is simple: fewer surprises, better decisions, and growing trust—both within and outside your organization.

READER'S TOOLKIT — REDUCE RISK, INCREASE TRUST

Before launch:

- What is the user impact if the system is wrong?
- Where is human review required, and how is it documented?

During pilot:

- Are we testing on real cases and monitoring by group?
- What did we learn, and what changed?
- After deployment:
- Who owns ongoing performance checks?
- How do users raise concerns, and how fast do we respond?

Responsible AI is not about saying "no" to technology; it is about saying "yes" to technology that protects people and delivers results. With clear purpose, strong guardrails, and human-centered leadership, you can adopt AI confidently—and keep your team and customers at the center of every decision.

CHAPTER FIVE
AI's VISIONARY FUTURE: COLLABORATIVE PARTNERS IN PROGRESS

If you worry that AI might make your role or your business obsolete, you are asking the right question at the right time. The strongest path forward is not replacement; it is collaboration. The most durable advantage comes when AI systems remove friction and extend human capability, while people set direction, values, and accountability.

MORE INNOVATIVE INFRASTRUCTURE, SMARTER BUSINESS

AI is already helping create more reliable operations that every business depends on.

- Autonomous and assistive systems: In well-defined domains such as warehouses, ports, and fixed delivery routes, AI enhances logistics, safety, and predictability.
- Smart cities: Data-informed operations can optimize energy, public transit, and city services. For businesses, this means steadier utilities and fewer disruptions when transparency and public input are part of the design.

AI AS A TEAMMATE

In proposal operations and program delivery, I have observed a consistent pattern: technology is most effective when it eliminates repetitive tasks, allowing people to focus on strategy, clarity, and relationships. That is the model for the modern workplace.

- Productivity and focus: AI can draft baselines, summarize lengthy materials, and extract key points, enabling teams to allocate more time to judgment and value.
- Accelerated innovation: By identifying patterns in large datasets, AI can generate new ideas for products, services, and operations—provided domain experts stay involved to validate and guide decisions.

PROGRESS IN HEALTH AND WELLNESS

Partnerships between clinicians and AI are helping experts act sooner and more precisely.

- Earlier detection: AI-assisted review of medical images and data can help flag risks earlier, allowing clinicians to intervene sooner.
- Personalized care: Tools can support tailoring plans to individual context. Success still relies on rigorous validation, human oversight, and lessons learned from systems that underperformed in practice.

EXPANDING HUMAN CREATIVITY

Generative tools are not a threat to creativity; they are a new way to explore it.

- Creative co-pilots: Writers, artists, and designers can iterate more quickly and explore a broader range of options when they combine their talents with the right tools. Clear labeling and rights management build trust.
- Immersive learning: In education and therapy, AI can help create personalized virtual and augmented experiences. When grounded in evidence and designed with accessibility in mind, these environments can enhance engagement and outcomes.

GUIDING PRINCIPLES FOR A DURABLE FUTURE

Technology will evolve. Your principles can remain steady.

1. Begin with human needs. Define a genuine problem you're addressing for a customer or employee. Success criteria should focus on human outcomes, not just technical metrics.
2. Keep people accountable. AI is a tool. For consequential decisions, humans are responsible. Provide clear paths to review, correct, and appeal.
3. Demand transparency: document data sources, intended use, and known limits—test for performance, fairness, and reliability both before and after deployment.
4. Prioritize security and safety to protect data and models. Plan for misuse scenarios and develop quick response mechanisms. Make privacy and safety non-negotiable.

YOUR ACTION CHECKLIST

1. Use these questions as a quick gate before adopting or expanding an AI solution:
2. What specific human need does this system address, and how will we measure whether it helped?
3. What new risks could this introduce, and how will we detect, prevent, and respond to them?
4. Who is accountable for outcomes, and how can affected users request a review or correction of these outcomes?
5. What are the system's limits, and how will we communicate these limits to users?

AI's future is not a story about tools replacing people—it is a story about people leading with clarity. When we utilize AI to eliminate friction and enhance human judgment, we create more resilient teams, foster stronger customer trust, and businesses that adapt more quickly than the headlines change.

Conclusion
Charting Your Course with Confidence

I f you picked up this book worried about what AI means for your job or your business, I want you to finish it feeling differently: with clarity and momentum. AI is powerful, yes—and imperfect. That combination opens up space for leadership. Your leadership.

Throughout these chapters, we emphasized a straightforward idea: view AI as a tool that reduces friction and enhances human potential, while people determine direction, values, and accountability. When you base adoption on this perspective, you shift from fear to intentional action.

What You Now Know

- The shift is fundamental and manageable. Progress in AI has resulted from the alignment of data, computing power, and improved learning techniques over time. Understanding this pattern helps you plan calmly, rather than reacting to headlines.
- AI is strongest as a teammate.

- Use it to draft baselines, summarize, detect patterns, and surface options—so people can focus on judgment, strategy, and relationships.
- Guardrails protect people and performance. Bias, privacy, and brittleness become manageable when you define purpose, keep humans involved, test in your environment, and make accountability clear.
- A simple framework wins: Understand – Question – Act (UQA)
- UQA keeps you in control: know what the system does, ask how and why, then move forward with safeguards and clear success criteria.

In my experience leading teams, success has come from mastering the basics: clear ownership, consistent processes, and prompt feedback. AI reduced friction, enabling people to deliver results more efficiently. That approach works everywhere.

Your Next 90 Days

For individuals

- Inventory your week: Identify two repetitive tasks you could safely offload to AI.
- Upskill with purpose: Select one tool that enhances your current role (summarization, drafting, analysis)—practice on low-risk tasks.
- Build your "proof" portfolio: Save examples where AI saved time or improved clarity. Show your impact.

For business owners and leaders

- Pick one process, not ten: Choose a stable, high-volume workflow (e.g., customer intake, FAQs, internal knowledge search) and pilot AI with human review.
- Stand up a small content library: Curate your best templates, past wins, and FAQs. Tag for reuse.
- Define ownership and review: Assign a human owner and document when and how reviews happen before anything reaches customers.
- Close the loop: After 30 days, gather lessons learned and update templates. Minor improvements repeated lead to success.

INDICATORS THAT YOU'RE ON TRACK

- Cycle time: Faster to a first, usable draft—without more rework downstream.
- Defect rate: Fewer compliance gaps and factual corrections at review.
- Reuse effectiveness: Approved content blocks decrease effort across teams.
- Alignment: Clear traceability from objectives to narrative and evidence.
- Trust: Colleagues and customers understand what AI supports—and what people own.

CULTURE THAT OUTLASTS THE HYPE

- People first: Define success in human terms—clarity, safety, equity, value.
- Accountability by design: Tools assist; people remain responsible.
- Transparency: Say what the system does, where it helps, and where it stops.

- Learning loops: Each project gets better the next time. Document, share, refine.
- Security and privacy: Non-negotiable. Earn trust daily.

When I've led teams through change, the breakthrough wasn't a single tool—it was a shared operating rhythm: clear purpose, disciplined review, continuous improvement. AI helps that rhythm scale.

Reader's Toolkit — Final Checklist

- Purpose: What problem are we solving, and how will we measure success?
- People: Who is accountable? Where are the human checkpoints?
- Data: What's used, who can access it, and how is it protected?
- Performance: How does it behave on our real cases and sub-groups?
- Process: How will we monitor, retrain, and respond to drift or failure?
- Transparency: What do users need to know, and how do they expect to be informed?

AI isn't the end; it's what we create. The outcomes depend on your choices—what you adopt, how you implement, which problems you prioritize, and how you lead your team through the work. Start small, learn quickly, and expand what works. That is how you turn anxiety into an advantage—and build a future where the best of technology amplifies the best of people.

If you found this book helpful, I'd be very appreciative if you could leave a favorable review for it on Amazon.

Leave an Amazon Review

About the Author

Serial Entrepreneur | Federal Contracting Leader | AI Strategist | Exit Planning Mentor | Author

Dwayne Robinson is a nationally recognized entrepreneur and strategist with extensive expertise in IT, artificial intelligence, federal contracting, and mergers and acquisitions (M&A) strategy. He founded Vision Systems & Technology, Inc., a software engineering company in 1997, scaling it into a multi-million-dollar enterprise that supported the U.S. Intelligence Community and the Department of Defense, before successfully exiting through an acquisition by SAS in 2012.

He currently serves as Director of Business Operations at the University System of Maryland, where he manages a diverse portfolio of federal contracts and partnerships with agencies such as NASA, DoD, and the Veterans Administration. Dwayne is also the Founder of agentalis.ai, an advanced Agentic AI platform that provides users with easy access to specialized autonomous AI agents.

As an active mentor to founders and executives, Dwayne serves as a Senior Advisor at Executive Business Advisors and a TEDCO Network Advisor, guiding business owners through growth, operational transformation, and exit readiness. He is the author of *"Emerging AI Technology: A Glimpse into the Future"* and *"How to Start a Business: An 11-Step Guide to Help Aspiring Entrepreneurs Achieve Success and Financial Freedom."*

His achievements have earned him recognition as a Washington Tech Fast 50 honoree, Smart CEO Smart 100 CEO, and a Black Enterprise Small Business of the Year nominee. Dwayne offers unmatched insight, operational excellence, and forward-thinking vision to entrepreneurs ready to grow and build lasting companies.

GLOSSARY OF TERMS

A

Accountability — The principle of identifying who is responsible for the outcomes when AI systems are used, especially for high-impact decisions.

Accelerated innovation — The capability of AI to identify patterns in large datasets and generate new ideas for products, services, and operations, requiring domain expert validation.

AI winters — Historical periods when enthusiasm for intelligent machines cooled because expectations exceeded actual AI results.

Artificial Intelligence (AI) — A powerful tool designed to amplify human talent by automating repetitive tasks, allowing people to focus on strategy, creativity, and relationships.

Autonomous and assistive systems — AI systems that enhance logistics, safety, and predictability in specific, well-defined domains like warehouses or delivery routes.

B

Bias and unfairness — A typical risk pattern where AI models learn from historical data that reflects existing inequities, causing the system to reproduce or amplify those biases.

C

Change control — A safeguard that involves documenting and approving changes to AI components like prompts, training data, and content libraries, similar to managing code.

Clear user communication — A safeguard requiring transparency with users about AI-supported decisions and providing contact points for questions or appeals.

Climate and energy AI — AI applications used for forecasting and optimization, enabling more efficient management of energy systems and effective modeling of complex scenarios.

Conversational assistance — AI systems, such as voice and chat, that streamline customer support and internal workflows by handling routine inquiries and information lookups.

Creative co-pilots — Generative AI tools that assist humans like writers, artists, and designers in iterating faster and exploring a broader range of innovative options.

D

Data dependence — The characteristic that AI systems reflect the quality and nature of the training data they are given, meaning biased or incomplete data leads to flawed behavior.

Deep learning — A type of AI where models are trained on massive datasets to learn complex patterns in images, speech, and text.

Drift — The phenomenon where the performance of an AI system changes over time, requiring ongoing monitoring and potential retraining.

E

Earlier detection — The application of AI to review medical images and data to help flag risks sooner, enabling clinicians to intervene more promptly.

Education AI — AI applications such as adaptive learning and tutoring aids that support teachers and personalize instruction for students.

Ethics — The responsible use of AI, which requires careful attention to fairness, accountability, and meaningful human oversight beyond just technical accuracy.

Evidence and traceability — A safeguard that links AI claims to their sources and tracks model versions and content origins to ensure transparency and trust.

F

Financial services AI — AI applications used within financial sectors to detect fraud, assess economic risk, and strengthen security and operational efficiency.

G

Generalization — The ability of AI models to perform reliably when faced with real-world variations, beyond just the clean data they were trained and tested on.

Generative modeling — AI models that can synthesize new content like text, images, audio, and code, offering powerful capabilities for creativity and productivity while needing safeguards.

Governance — The structured process of establishing clarity and standards for AI adoption, encompassing roles, risk classification, review schedules, and training to ensure responsible use.

Guardrails — Responsible safeguards and a human-first mindset applied to AI to protect people, reduce surprises, and ensure the reliable delivery of benefits.

H

Healthcare support — AI algorithms that assist clinicians by spotting patterns in medical images and data, thereby augmenting human expert judgment.

Human-First Perspective — An approach to AI that focuses on using technology to eliminate low-value friction, allowing people to perform at their best and concentrate on strategic tasks.

Human-in-the-loop — The practice of intentionally keeping human oversight in critical AI workflows, requiring people to review, approve, or override AI decisions, especially for high-impact tasks.

I

Immersive learning — AI applications that create personalized virtual and augmented experiences in education and therapy, designed to enhance engagement and outcomes.

Interpretability — The degree to which a complex AI model's decisions and internal workings can be understood and explained, which is crucial for transparency and auditability in high-stakes applications.

M

Manufacturing and quality AI — AI applications, such as vision systems, that identify defects in real-time and predictive maintenance tools that minimize downtime in industrial settings.

Massive data — One of the three pillars of modern AI, referring to the vast quantities of digital content, sensor inputs, and connected device data used to train systems to learn robust patterns.

Misinformation — A risk pattern where generative AI systems produce fluent but factually incorrect content, requiring human review for accuracy.

Modern AI — The current era of artificial intelligence that emerged when massive data, powerful computing resources, and more innovative training methods aligned, enabling practical tools.

O

Opacity and accountability — A risk where AI's "black-box" nature makes it challenging to explain decisions, necessitating clear ownership, detailed records, and defined appeal processes for users.

Overconfidence — A risk where predictive AI systems, despite performing well in testing, can be brittle and fail under new, real-world conditions.

P

Personalized care — AI tools that help tailor plans to individual contexts, particularly in healthcare, always relying on rigorous human oversight and validation.

Powerful compute — One of the three pillars of modern AI, referring to specialized hardware like GPUs that enable the training of deeper, more capable AI models at scale.

Privacy — A critical risk area concerning the protection of sensitive information involved in AI training and deployment, requiring strong data protection and governance.

Problem-first scoping — A practical safeguard that ensures each AI use case is tied to a specific, measurable outcome, prompting a pause if the objective is vague.

Productivity and focus — AI's ability to automate repetitive tasks like drafting or summarizing, thereby allowing human teams to dedicate more time to judgment, strategy, and value-added work.

R

Real-world testing — A safeguard involving piloting AI systems with actual data and workflows, measuring performance across diverse scenarios and user groups, and monitoring for performance changes.

Recommendations and personalization — AI applications used by platforms to tailor customer experiences by suggesting content or products, balancing personalization with user control.

Reinforcement learning — A type of AI where systems learn to master complex tasks through trial and error, informing advancements in areas like robotics and operations.

Responsible AI — The holistic approach of adopting AI confidently by integrating clear purpose, strong guardrails, and human-centered leadership to protect people and deliver beneficial results.

Review cadence — A governance practice that involves scheduling periodic checks (e.g., quarterly) to reassess an AI system's performance, fairness, security, and user feedback.

Risk management — The strategic process of acknowledging and designing safeguards for AI risks early to protect people, brand, and operations, ensuring reliable benefits.

Risk tiering — A governance practice of classifying AI uses based on their potential impact (e.g., on people, finances, safety) to determine the necessary level of oversight and documentation.

Robustness — The ability of AI models to maintain high performance and reliability even when encountering variations or unexpected conditions in real-world environments.

Roles and responsibilities — A governance element that assigns specific human owners for each AI use, who are then responsible for approving its purpose, data sources, and deployment criteria.

S

Safety — A non-negotiable aspect of responsible AI use, requiring attention to ensure systems operate without causing harm and include meaningful human oversight.

Security — A non-negotiable aspect of AI use that mandates strong data protection and governance to prevent sensitive information from being exposed or misused.

Smart cities — Data-informed AI operations that optimize public services such as energy, transit, and city management, leading to greater efficiency and fewer disruptions.

More innovative training methods — One of the three pillars of modern AI, referring to improved learning techniques and architectures that led to significant advancements in areas like vision, speech, and language tasks.

T

Transformer architectures — A significant advance in AI that revolutionized how systems understand and generate human language, forming the foundation for many modern language tools.

Transparency — A guiding principle that demands documentation of data sources, intended use, known limits, and testing results for performance, fairness, and reliability of AI systems.

Training and awareness — A governance element focused on educating and equipping teams to use AI responsibly through examples and clear guidance.

Transportation and logistics AI — AI applications, such as route optimization and traffic prediction, that offer a competitive advantage for businesses involved in moving goods.

U

Understand–Question–Act (UQA) — A simple operating model and framework designed to help individuals and businesses confidently adopt AI by first understanding a system, then questioning its details, and finally acting responsibly.

V

Vision breakthroughs — Landmark advancements in image recognition that have enabled robust visual understanding for applications like quality control and medical imaging support.

References

Financial Stability Board. (2017). Financial stability implications of artificial intelligence and machine learning. Financial Stability Board. https://www.fsb.org/2017/11/artificial-intelligence-and-machine-learning-in-financial-service/

Fuster, A., Goldsmith-Pinkham, P., Ramadorai, T., & Walther, A. (2022). Predictably unequal? The effects of machine learning on credit markets. The Journal of Finance, 77(1), 5–47. https://doi.org/10.1111/jofi.13090

Gulshan, V., Peng, L., Coram, M., Stumpe, M. C., Wu, D., Narayanaswamy, A., Venugopalan, S., Widner, K., Madams, T., Cuadros, J., Kim, R., Raman, R., Nelson, P. C., Mega, J. L., & Webster, D. R. (2016). Development and validation of a deep learning algorithm for detection of diabetic retinopathy in retinal fundus photographs. JAMA, 316(22), 2402–2410. https://doi.org/10.1001/jama.2016.17216

Ipp, E., Liljenquist, D., Bode, B., Shah, V. N., Silverstein, S., Regillo, C. D., Lim, J. I., Sadda, S., Domalpally, A., Gray, G., Bhaskaranand, M., Ramachandra, C., & Solanki, K. (2021). Pivotal evaluation of an artificial intelligence system for autonomous detection of referrable and vision-threatening diabetic retinopathy. JAMA Network Open, 4(11), e2134254. https://doi.org/10.1001/jamanetworkopen.2021.34254

National Institute of Standards and Technology. (2023). Artificial Intelligence Risk Management Framework (AI RMF 1.0) (NIST AI 100-1). National Institute of Standards and Technology. https://doi.org/10.6028/NIST.AI.100-1

OECD. (2019). OECD employment outlook 2019: The future of work. OECD Publishing. https://doi.org/10.1787/9ee00155-en

Obermeyer, Z., Powers, B., Vogeli, C., & Mullainathan, S. (2019). Dissecting racial bias in an algorithm used to manage the health of populations. Science, 366(6464), 447–453. https://doi.org/10.1126/science.aax2342

Recht, B., Roelofs, R., Schmidt, L., & Shankar, V. (2018). Do CIFAR-10 classifiers generalize to CIFAR-10? arXiv. https://arxiv.org/abs/1806.00451

Ross, C., & Swetlitz, I. (2018, July 25). IBM Watson recommended unsafe, incorrect treatments. STAT. https://www.statnews.com/2018/07/25/ibm-watson-recommended-unsafe-incorrect-treatments/

Rudin, C. (2019). Stop explaining black box machine learning models for high-stakes decisions and use interpretable models instead. Nature Machine Intelligence, 1, 206–215. https://doi.org/10.1038/s42256-019-0048-x

World Economic Forum. (2023). Future of jobs report 2023. https://www.wefo
rum.org/reports/the-future-of-jobs-report-2023/